Oman

Travel guide 2024

A Comprehensive Travel Guide for Cultural Exploration, Adventure Expeditions, and Seamless Journeys

By: JOHN C. HILL

Travel guide to oman 2024

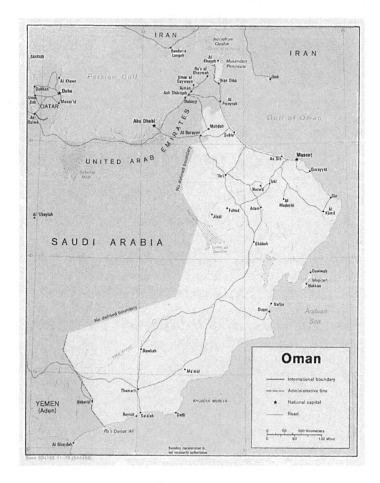

Oman map

Table of contents

Copyright

1.INTRODUCTION

Immerse yourself in the rich tapestry of history, culture, and scenic beauty of Oman, a gem located on the southeast corner of the Arabian Peninsula. This guide acts as a doorway to the stunning scenery and inviting atmosphere that 2024 has to offer tourists.

1.1 A Synopsis of Oman

Oman, formally the Sultanate of Oman, is a prime example of how tradition and modernization may coexist together. Oman, which is sandwiched between Yemen, Saudi Arabia, and the United Arab Emirates, has a varied terrain that includes sweeping deserts, breathtaking mountains, and an immaculate Arabian Sea shoreline.

Muscat, the capital, acts as a center of the economy and culture. Its whitewashed structures with traditional Islamic architecture form a mesmerizing fusion of modern beauty and old-world charm. The painstaking preservation of historic landmarks, including the old city of Nizwa and the strong forts that dot the terrain, is evidence of Oman's dedication to maintaining its cultural legacy.

Oman's natural treasures may be found outside its metropolitan areas. With Jebel Shams, the "Mountain of the Sun," as the highest point in the nation, the untamed Hajar Mountains provide stunning views. The Wahiba Sands, on the other hand, are an unending expanse of golden dunes that enthrall the spirit of adventure.

The beauty of Oman's coastline cannot be ignored. The nation provides a wide variety of aquatic experiences, from the calm beaches along the Salalah coast to the crystal-clear seas of the Daymaniyat Islands. Explore colorful coral reefs, see the fascinating green turtles that nest at Ras Al Jinz, or just relax on fine beaches under the Arabian sun.

1.2 Travel Advice and Important Details

To guarantee a smooth and rewarding trip, careful planning is necessary before departing for Oman. The following are crucial travel advice to improve your exploration:

Visa Requirements: Read up on Oman's visa regulations before you pack your luggage. Most nations may get a tourist visa on arrival, but it's important to make sure you comply with entrance requirements and check the most recent changes.

The best time to visit Oman is in the summer when temperatures soar, and in the winter, when temperatures are moderate. The milder months of October through April are the best times to go since the weather is more conducive to outdoor activities.

Local Transportation: Oman is accessible by automobile thanks to its well-kept road system. Renting a car gives you the freedom to go to far-off places. As alternatives, there are public buses and taxis available; Muscat has a dependable public transit network.

Cultural Sensitivity: It's important to respect regional traditions. Wear modest clothing, particularly when you're in places of worship. Minimal public demonstrations of love are advised, and alcohol should only be used in establishments that are authorized.

Language and Communication: Although English is widely understood, particularly in metropolitan areas, Arabic is the official language. Nonetheless, picking up a few simple Arabic words may improve your relationships with people and your understanding of their culture.

Health and Safety: Oman places a high priority on safety, although common sense safeguards must be followed. Use sunblock, drink plenty of water, and use caution while in a desert area. Major cities in the nation have state-of-the-art healthcare facilities, making it a respected system.

Money & Money Matters: The national currency is the Omani Rial (OMR). Although credit cards are often accepted, it's a good idea to have extra cash on hand, particularly in more isolated locations. ATMs are widely available in cities.

Connectivity: Oman has a solid infrastructure for telecommunications. Visitors may easily get local SIM cards, which provide quick access to communication and data services.

In conclusion, Oman entices visitors with a wide range of experiences, from tranquility in unspoiled landscapes to historic customs in busy souqs. Equipped with these travel suggestions, go off on an adventure that guarantees not only amazing vistas but also a profound bond with this Arabian treasure's heart and soul.

2. GETTING THERE

Understanding the complexities of local travel customs, visa procedures, and transportation is essential to seeing Oman's captivating landscapes. This section provides a thorough overview to guarantee a smooth trip from arrival to exploring.

2.1 Options for Transportation

Air Travel: Muscat International Airport, a state-of-the-art facility providing a seamless entrance into the country, is Oman's main gateway. Muscat is accessible from major international centers thanks to connections made by airlines from all over the globe. Another access point is the Salalah International Airport in the south.

Road Travel: Oman borders Yemen, Saudi Arabia, and the United Arab Emirates, making it a great place for anybody looking for an overland journey. Having border crossings and well-maintained highways makes driving easier. Renting a car gives you the flexibility to see the various landscapes at your speed.

Sea Travel: Due to Oman's extensive coastline, sea travel has a long history. Although contemporary cruise ships often call in Muscat, traditional dhows continue to sail the seas, providing a distinctive viewpoint of Oman's breathtaking coastline.

2.2 Requirements for Visas

It's essential to comprehend Oman's visa regulations for seamless admission. For most nations, Oman normally provides a simple visa-on-arrival scheme as of 2024. But it's important to keep abreast of any modifications to the rules and regulations.

Visa-On-Arrival: Upon arrival at Muscat International Airport or other entry points, a lot of people may get a visa. The length of stay varies, usually lasting between ten days and a month. Verify the most recent restrictions and the validity of your passport.

E-Visa: Travelers may apply for a visa online in Oman and get it in advance of their trip. This might be a practical choice as it makes admission requirements clear and streamlines the arrival procedure.

Packages for Tourist e-Visas: Take into account looking at tourist e-Visas that might contain other services like travel and hotel reservations.

These travel packages simplify the trip planning process and provide guests with a full range of options.

2.3 Advice on Local Transportation

Oman's wide-ranging scenery and array of attractions make efficient local transportation essential. Traveling is much more enjoyable when one knows what alternatives are available and some helpful hints for getting about.

Renting a vehicle: Hiring a vehicle is a popular way to see Oman because of the country's well-maintained highways and obvious signs. Airports and large cities are home to rental firms that provide a variety of vehicles. This adaptability is especially helpful for those heading into the untamed areas of the Wahiba Sands or the rocky Hajar Mountains.

Taxis: Taxis are easily found in cities and may be reserved via ride-hailing applications or by hailing one on the street. Even if they are a practical choice for short trips, it is best to settle on the fee in advance of the trip.

Public Buses: Major districts in Muscat are connected by a dependable public bus system. This is a reasonably priced choice for individuals who are on a tight budget. In more isolated locations, the coverage can be less, thus it's important to confirm the schedule in advance.

Private Tours and Transfers: Take into account private tours or transfers for a more specialized experience. In addition to transportation, these services provide insights from experienced guides who may give historical narratives and cultural backgrounds.

Internal Flights: Because of the size of the nation, internal travel might save a lot of time. Travelers who are visiting many locations might cut down on their journey time by using domestic flights that link Muscat with Salalah and other regional airports.

When using public transit in Oman, it's important to know the customs and protocol. Being on time is expected, and a courteous attitude toward other passengers and drivers enhances the experience. Accepting the beat of Oman's transportation improves the experience whether you're traveling through busy city streets or peaceful desert stretches.

In summary, a combination of meticulous preparation and flexibility is needed to become an expert in the art of traveling to and within Oman. Oman extends a warm welcome to visitors, offering a journey beyond convention and time, from the sky to the roads and the seas.

3. ACCOMODATIONS

Oman's charm is not limited to its picturesque scenery; it also includes the warmth of its lodgings. Oman's lodging options include luxurious hotels as well as affordable resorts, satisfying a wide range of preferences. This section explores lodging and provides useful guidance to enhance your visit to this Arabian treasure.

3.1 Overview of Hotels and Resorts

The hotels and resorts in Oman are the perfect example of how to combine contemporary comfort with traditional charm. There are several types of accommodations available in the nation, ranging from opulent urban hideouts to picturesque coastline getaways.

Muscat's Luxurious Enclaves: The capital city of Muscat creates an opulent atmosphere. Elegant accommodations, including The Chedi Muscat and Al Bustan Palace, A Ritz-Carlton Hotel, redefine luxury with their top-notch facilities, flawless service, and striking architecture. With views of the Gulf of Oman's crystal-clear seas, these accommodations provide a sanctuary for sophisticated tourists yearning for sophistication.

Coastal Retreats: Resorts like Shangri-La Barr Al Jissah Resort & Spa and Six Senses Zighy Bay provide exclusive havens along the immaculate coastline. Tucked up amid craggy cliffs, these hideaways provide exclusive access to private beaches, spas, and fine dining experiences. The visitor experience is enhanced by the coastline environment, which offers amazing views from every angle.

Desert Oasis Retreats: For travelers captivated by the ethereal charm of the deserts, Desert Nights Camp and Dunes by Al Nahda provide a distinctive fusion of luxury and genuineness. In the center of the Wahiba Sands, contemporary conveniences combined with traditional Bedouin-style tents provide a strange experience. Around the campfire, guests may enjoy stargazing, camel rides at dusk, and traditional Omani food.

3.2 Inexpensive Choices

Budget-conscious tourists are welcome in Oman, where a variety of lodging options emphasize cost without sacrificing comfort.

These choices guarantee that the cost of exploration won't be prohibitive.

Guesthouses and Budget Hotels: For travelers looking for affordable lodging, Muscat and other cities offer a wide selection of guesthouses and budget hotels. Some budget-friendly accommodations that provide tidy, pleasant rooms include the Al Falaj Hotel and Safeer Hotel. These lodgings frequently offer needed facilities and a strategic location for comfortable exploring.

Hostels & Backpacker Lodges: Located in Salalah and Muscat, these establishments provide a shared environment for budget-conscious and lone travelers alike. For example, Youth Hostel Muscat offers an affordable choice with shared dorms and common areas that encourage socializing among tourists who have similar interests.

Local Guest Experiences: In rural locations, think about homestays or local guesthouses for a genuinely immersive and affordable experience. These actively support the local economy in addition to offering a look at Omani hospitality. Through websites like Airbnb, tourists may discover hidden treasures and establish friendships with locals, gaining insights into the real Omani way of life.

3.3 Distinctive Visits and Small Hotels

Oman's charm goes beyond standard lodging, allowing visitors to partake in memorable stays that enhance the whole experience. Unique accommodations and boutique hotels provide a customized experience that guarantees experiences that go beyond the typical.

ancient Retreats: By renting rooms in repurposed ancient structures, you may fully immerse yourself in Oman's colorful history. The Falaj Daris Hotel in Nizwa skillfully combines the allure of an old fort with modern luxury. These lodgings provide guests with a trip through Oman's rich cultural legacy in addition to a comfortable getaway.

Mountaintop Getaways: Nestled above mountains, the Hajar Mountains provide distinctive havens. Alila Jabal Akhdar, for instance, blends luxury with stunning views. These intimate lodgings provide privacy so that visitors may enjoy peace of mind among the untamed splendor of Oman's highlands.

Eco-Friendly Retreats: Eco-friendly lodgings demonstrate Oman's dedication to environmentally responsible travel. The View blends in well with the natural surroundings of the Al Jabal Al Akhdar area. These retreats place a high value on protecting the environment without sacrificing the quality of the visitor experience.

To sum up, Oman's lodging options serve a wide range of visitors, guaranteeing that every trip is unique and unforgettable. Whether bathing in luxury, embracing budget-friendly alternatives, or relishing in unusual stays, the lodgings of Oman form a vital part of the traveler's story, weaving together comfort, culture, and discovery.

4. CULTURAL INSIGHT

Oman invites visitors to explore its diverse cultural fabric, where ancient customs coexist peacefully with contemporary life. This section explores Oman's history, language, traditions, and the colorful tapestry of festivals that define the country's character, providing a helpful starting point for understanding the country's subtle cultural subtleties.

4.1 Oman's Varied Traditions and History

Historical Tapestry: Bedouin customs, maritime commerce, and a key geopolitical location are all interwoven throughout Oman's colorful past. The nation's historical importance is shown by the frankincense trade routes, the UNESCO-listed Bahla Fort, and the ancient port city of Qalhat. Visitors may go back in time to the Sultanate to see architectural treasures, which include the mud-brick dwellings of Al Hamra and the fort of Nizwa.

The Frankincense Trail, a UNESCO World Heritage Site, honors Oman's historical significance as a major participant in the incense trade. Along this path, visitors may discover historic ports and cities, such as the port city of Khor Rori and the archaeological site of Sumhuram. The rich history of frankincense is unveiled, highlighting its significance for the local economy and culture.

Bedouin history: Bedouin villages in the Wahiba Sands of Oman continue to live according to their traditional ways, preserving their nomadic Bedouin history. Experience the hospitality of these people who live in the desert and learn about their traditions, food, and skill of negotiating the enormous dunes. The tale of Oman gains a depth of cultural complexity from the genuineness of the Bedouin way of life.

4.2 Vernacular and Traditions

Arabic as a Cultural Pillar: Although English is commonly spoken, learning some basic Arabic phrases enriches the cultural experience. Arabic is the official language of Oman. Making bonds with locals is facilitated by greeting them with "As-salaam alaikum" (Peace be upon you) and expressing thanks with "Shukran". A greater understanding of Oman's cultural legacy is reflected in the respect for the language.

Customs and Courtesies: Omani society lays significant significance on civility and hospitality. It is normal to provide a kind greeting and carry on a courteous conversation with people. Wearing modest clothing is preferred while visiting houses or places of worship. Sincere curiosity in Omani traditions, like the Majlis (a traditional meeting place), demonstrates cultural sensitivity and promotes deep connections.

Culinary Traditions: The rich and varied history of Oman has left its mark on the delicious fusion of tastes found in its cuisine. The nation's Bedouin and marine background is reflected in the usage of spices, dates, and fragrant rice. Tasting regional specialties like (slow-cooked marinated beef) and Omani halwa transforms dining into a cultural adventure that reflects the variety of the nation.

4.3 Celebrations & Occasions

National Day Celebrations: November 18th is Oman's National Day, a joyous celebration commemorating the Sultanate's independence. Parades, fireworks, and cultural activities showcasing Oman's pride and solidarity are all part of the festivities. Visitors get a peek at the country's modern character via the colorful display of the national flag and the festive ambiance.

Muscat Festival: The capital city comes alive with culture every year at the Muscat Festival. Exhibitions of art, dance, and traditional music highlight Oman's rich creative legacy. The festival offers a wide range of cultural activities that enthrall both residents and tourists, from contemporary art exhibits to camel racing.

Eid Al-Fitr and Eid Al-Adha: These two important Islamic holidays unite communities via their celebratory nature. Eid Al-Fitr celebrates the completion of Ramadan, the holy month of fasting, while Eid Al-Adha honors Ibrahim's sacrifice. Oman is merry at these holidays, with family getting together, having meals together, and doing charitable deeds.

On July 23, we commemorate the reign of Sultan Qaboos bin Said, which is known as Renaissance Day. Parades, cultural activities, and patriotic displays honoring Oman's contemporary age of prosperity and development are held on this day. This is a unique opportunity to experience the Sultanate's modern story.

In summary, Oman's cultural environment is a patchwork of historic customs and modern vitality. Taking part in the nation's festivities, honoring traditions, and embracing the historical journey provide visitors with an immersive experience that goes beyond simple observation. Adventurers are urged by Oman's cultural insights to immerse themselves in the country's ongoing story, rather than just visiting.

5. MUST SEE ATTRACTIONS

Oman entices visitors with a wide range of must-see sites. It is a treasure trove of natural beauty and cultural treasures. This book reveals five treasures that perfectly capture Oman's charm, ranging from breathtaking architectural feats to immaculate natural settings.

5.1 The Grand Mosque of Sultan Qaboos

In the center of Muscat, the Sultan Qaboos Grand Mosque is a famous landmark that attests to Oman's architectural skill and cultural diversity. The mosque, named after Sultan Qaboos bin Said, the visionary leader who was instrumental in Oman's Renaissance, is a masterwork of Islamic architecture.

Architectural Splendor: As tourists approach the mosque's meticulously sculpted facade, they are struck by its majesty. The main prayer hall is a stunning display of artistry, complete with a large chandelier and a handmade carpet that covers the whole space. Admirers and worshippers alike are drawn to the peaceful atmosphere created by the tasteful fusion of Omani, Indian, and Persian architectural forms.

Courtyard & Gardens: The spacious courtyard offers a peaceful area for reflection with its well-kept gardens and reflecting ponds. There is a feeling of tranquility emanating from the mosque's white marble surfaces as they sparkle in the Omani sun. Oman's dedication to maintaining its cultural legacy is seen in the careful attention to detail in both the building and design.

Cultural Significance: The Sultan Qaboos Grand Mosque is a center for intercultural understanding in addition to being a work of architectural wonder. Visitors who are not Muslims are invited to see the mosque and learn about Islamic customs. It invites people from all walks of life to enjoy its beauty and importance as a beacon of religious tolerance.

5.2 The Akhdar Jabal

Jabal Akhdar, which translates as "Green Mountain," is a rough and striking mountain range located in the Al Hajar Mountains of Oman. Jabal Akhdar, well-known for its mild weather, terraced fields, and breathtaking views, provides a welcome diversion from the dry lowlands.

tiered Agriculture: Omani farmers' inventiveness is on display in the mountain's tiered landscape, which was chiseled into the rocks over generations. In this hilltop paradise, fragrant herbs, rose gardens, and fruit orchards flourish. In addition to enjoying the local food, which includes pomegranates, apricots, and roses used to make Omani rose water, visitors may see traditional agricultural methods in action.

Rose Harvesting Season: Usually taking place in April, this is one of Jabal Akhdar's most charming times of the year. The terraced fields become a sea of pink flowers as the exquisite aroma of Damask roses fills the air. This natural wonder is celebrated every year with the Rose Festival, which allows attendees to participate in cultural events and buy locally produced rose-themed goods.

Points of Interest: Jabal Akhdar is home to several scenic sites that provide expansive views of the neighboring valleys and mountains. One such location that offers a spectacular view of the canyon below is Diana's Point, named after Princess Diana who made visits to the region. These vantage locations are perfect for seeing how the countryside changes color at dawn and dusk.

5.3 The Sands of Wahiba

The immense sea of dunes that stretches over central Oman is called the Wahiba Sands, or Sharqiya Sands. The captivating sight of this always-changing desert terrain beckons visitors to discover the peace and splendor of the Omani desert.

Dune Bashing and Camel Trekking: Wahiba Sands provides thrilling dune bashing experiences for those seeking adventure. Expert drivers maneuver around the high dunes, making for an exhilarating ride. An alternative is to go on a camel trek, which offers a more tranquil exploring experience since you can interact with the ancient desert landscape via the rhythmic footfall of these desert animals.

Desert Camps: For those looking for an authentic experience, spending a night in a traditional desert camp is a must. Under the starry desert sky, contemporary comforts furnished in Bedouin-style tents provide a cozy haven. Enjoy authentic Omani food, take part in stargazing activities, and listen to traditional music.

Sunset Magic: Particularly at dawn and sunset, the shifting sands provide an ever-changing painting. Wahiba Sands becomes a bizarre scene as the sun casts warm colors across the dunes. The quiet of the desert and the gracefully sloping dunes there are a source of comfort for both nature lovers and photographers.

5.4 Mutrah Souq

Located on Old Muscat's corniche, Mutrah Souq is a vibrant marketplace that perfectly captures Omani trade and craftsmanship. Discover the colorful fabrics, spices, and handicrafts lining the small lanes of this authentic souq, which offers an immersive experience.

Customary Omani Items: The Mutrah Souq is a veritable gold mine of Omani artistry. Among the many things for sale are silver jewelry, ceramics, intricately woven carpets, and traditional Omani Khanjars, or ceremonial daggers. The genuineness of the souq and the artistry of its sellers make for an unforgettable shopping experience.

Fish Market and Corniche: The Muttrah Fish Market, which is next to the souq, offers a window into Oman's nautical history via the sounds and sights of fishermen hauling in their catch. Magnificent views of the sea, the Mutrah Fort, and the famous incense burner monument may be seen from the waterfront corniche. This walkway along the shore offers a calm contrast to the bustling souq.

5.5 Muscat's Royal Opera House

A cultural gem in the center of the city, Oman's Royal Opera House Muscat is proof of the country's dedication to the arts and its thriving cultural landscape. Since its opening in 2011, the opera house has emerged as a leading venue for both modern and traditional performances.

Architectural Elegance: The opera house's architecture expertly combines Islamic and Omani elements to produce an edifice of unmatched beauty. With its magnificent dome and elaborate carvings, the building's grandeur is a work of visual art. The way that contemporary conveniences are mixed with traditional aesthetics shows how committed Oman is to protecting its history while looking to the future.

Cultural Events: A wide variety of events, including ballet, opera, classical music, and traditional Omani arts, are held at the Royal Opera House. Globally recognized performers frequent its stages, drawing in art fans from all corners of the globe. The opera house's dedication to cross-cultural communication and cooperation is a reflection of Oman's global perspective.

Beautifully designed planted grounds around the opera house, offer a calm area for reflection and relaxation. The venue's cultural importance is complemented by the harmonious setting created by the mix of water features, sculptures, and plants.

In conclusion, a look into the many dimensions of Oman's cultural and natural beauty may be had at these must-see locations. Each location adds to the complex story of this fascinating nation, from architectural wonders and mountain getaways to colorful souqs and desert vistas. Discovering these jewels offers a deep connection to Oman's spirit in addition to a visual feast.

6. ADVENTURE AND OUTDOOR ACTIVITIES

Adventurers will find an outdoor playground in Oman's various landscapes, which include enormous deserts, stunning coasts, and steep mountains. This article reveals five thrilling activities that perfectly capture Oman's adventurous character.

6.1 The Shab of Wadi

Adventure seekers and lovers of the great outdoors will find paradise in Wadi Shab, a ACTIVITIES

gorgeous canyon oasis tucked between sheer rocks. Wadi Shab, which is close to the seaside resort of Tiwi, provides a variety of hiking, swimming, and exploring experiences.

Hiking Through Palms: Getting to Wadi Shab involves a gorgeous boat trip, which is followed by a climb through rocky areas and palm plantations. As the route meanders by emerald-green lakes, one can't help but be excited about what is to come. In addition to taking in the natural beauty of the surroundings, visitors may see local fauna.

Swimming Through Caverns: Swimming through crystal-clear lakes and caverns is one of Wadi Shab's attractions. The explorers come into a sequence of wet rooms as they go down into the wadi. Those who risk the swim will be rewarded with a spectacular vista of the pouring water against the rocky background as they reach the finish, where a secret waterfall waits.

Wadi Shab Village Cultural Encounter: Traveling to Wadi Shab often entails traveling through charming Omani villages. These interactions provide a window into rural life and a chance to establish a connection with the locals. The friendliness of the locals gives the encounter a cultural twist and completes the Wadi Shab experience.

6.2 Shams of Jebel

The tallest peak in the Al Hajar mountain range, Jebel Shams, sometimes referred to as the "Mountain of the Sun," entices hikers and thrill-seekers with its rough terrain. For those looking for a more strenuous experience, Jebel Shams is a must-visit location because of the amazing views from the peak and the difficult paths.

Grand Canyon of Arabia: Jebel Shams' most famous feature is the magnificent Wadi Ghul, often known as the "Grand Canyon of Arabia." Its towering cliffs descend to incredible depths, exposing a geological wonder sculpted by the powers of nature. Trekking along the canyon rim offers unmatched vistas of the untamed terrain underneath.

The Balcony Walk: Those seeking adventure may go out on this strenuous trek that hugs the canyon's brink. Hikers will experience a dizzying feeling of adventure as they wind along tight paths with expansive vistas of the abyss on this thrilling excursion. It feels both humble and amazing to be standing on the brink of the canyon and looking down at such a wide chasm.

Stargazing in Jebel Shams: Jebel Shams is a great place to stargaze because of the clean mountain air and low levels of light pollution. A celestial show emerges as the sun sets behind the rugged peaks, displaying a blanket of stars against the background of the black mountains. The experience gains a cosmic dimension while camping under the stars.

6.3 Daymaniyat Islands Diving

The protected marine reserve of the Daymaniyat Islands, which is close to Muscat, is a haven for undersea aficionados, with a thriving marine ecology full of colorful fish, coral reefs, and other marine life. Immersion diving in the Daymaniyat Islands' immaculate waters is a breathtaking experience that reveals the splendor of Oman's underwater ecosystem.

Rich Marine Biodiversity: The Daymaniyat Islands are known for having an abundance of marine life, which makes them a diver's dream come true. The underwater environment is home to colorful coral formations, coral gardens, and a variety of marine life, such as reef sharks, rays, and turtles. The warm waters and good visibility make this a perfect place to explore.

Diverse Dive Sites: Several dive sites on the islands can accommodate divers of all ability levels. Divers may choose experiences based on their level of competence, ranging from shallow coral gardens to deeper reef cliffs. Popular locations for seeing exquisite coral formations and schools of tropical fish include the Coral Garden and Aquarium.

Protection & Conservation: Oman's dedication to conservation is shown by the Daymaniyat Islands' designation as a marine reserve. It is recommended that divers use appropriate diving procedures to minimize their influence on the fragile marine habitat. This dedication to sustainability guarantees that Daymaniyat Islands' underwater marvels will be appreciated for decades to come.

6.4 Wahiba Sands Desert Safari

A spectacular desert safari is what adventure seekers are invited to experience at Wahiba Sands, a huge sea of undulating golden dunes. The Wahiba Sands is a classic Omani trip because of the dunes' rhythmic movement, the desert's untamed beauty, and the cultural encounters there.

Sandboarding and Dune Bashing: Wahiba Sands desert safaris often include dune bashing, an exhilarating activity in which drivers maneuver the sharply inclined dunes with accuracy. Sandboarding offers a chance to glide down the dunes and experience the excitement of the desert terrain for those looking for a more active trip.

Experience in a Traditional Bedouin Camp: A visit to a traditional Bedouin camp is a common component of Wahiba Sands desert excursions. Visitors may enjoy camel rides, traditional music, and friendly Omani hospitality while immersed in the Bedouin way of life here. Travelers can connect with the ageless soul of the desert via the enchanting atmosphere created by the campfires beneath the starry desert sky.

Stargazing in the Desert: Wahiba Sands provides an unmatched stargazing experience due to its isolated position and low levels of light pollution. The desert becomes a cosmic theater as the sun sets over the dunes. A sensation of amazement and wonder is evoked by the rare chance to see the Milky Way and constellations while camping outside.

6.5 Ras Al Jinz Turtle Watching

Ras Al Jinz, on the easternmost point of the Arabian Peninsula, is well known for being a green turtle hatching area. For those who love the outdoors, this seaside refuge offers a once-in-a-lifetime chance to see the age-old custom of turtle nesting and hatching.

Turtle Nesting Season: Green turtles come to Ras Al Jinz's sandy beaches during the nesting season, which usually lasts from June to September. To deposit their eggs, female turtles creep ashore under the cover of darkness. Seeing this magnificent process in action is a unique and humble experience that helps guests understand the age-old cycle of life.

Ras Al Jinz provides guided excursions for turtle viewing to cause as little disruption as possible to the turtles that are breeding. Visitors are led by experts to specific viewing locations so they may have a close-up look at the turtles without worrying about upsetting them. The trips provide informative perspectives on the conservation initiatives aimed at safeguarding critically endangered green turtles.

Hatchling Releases: From August through November, when the hatchlings are due to go into the sea, visitors may see the beautiful spectacle of little turtles making their way to the ocean. Programs for conservation in Ras Al Jinz work to safeguard the eggs and make sure the hatchlings have a safe voyage, which helps to preserve this threatened species.

To sum up, Oman's outdoor and adventure activities provide a wide variety of experiences, from diving into rich marine environments and seeing ancient turtle ceremonies to visiting canyon oases and climbing towering hills. Every journey adds to the diverse mosaic of Oman's natural treasures and allows visitors to see the wild side of the nation.

7. CULINARY DELIGHTS

Oman's cuisine is a balanced blend of local specialties, cultural influences, and a wide variety of flavorful spices. This book dives into the essence of Omani cuisine, highlighting its variety of dishes, street food favorites, and the subtle cultural aspects of eating that make traveling to Oman for food a pleasurable experience.

7.1 Overview of Omani Cuisine

The rich history of Oman is reflected in its cuisine, which combines Arabian, Persian, and Indian tastes with local ingredients. Omani cuisine entices the senses with a symphony of textures and flavors, supported by the abundance of the sea, the richness of date palms, and the aromatic spices of the souqs.

Seafood Extravaganza: Oman's cuisine heavily emphasizes seafood due to the country's long coastline. A careful combination of herbs and spices is often used while preparing fish, shrimp, and lobster. Showcasing the freshness of the catch, grilled fish flavored with Omani rubs and served with aromatic rice is a classic meal.

Rice as a Staple: Rice, frequently seasoned with fragrant spices like saffron and cardamom, is the cornerstone of many Omani meals. The rice is cooked to a precise texture and taste balance by careful preparation. Omani rice dishes are a delectable culinary treat when paired with different meats, veggies, or seafood.

Dates and Date Products: Omani culture and cuisine are fundamentally based on dates. Date palms around the country produce a wide range of date varieties, each with a distinct taste character. Dates are utilized in both savory and sweet recipes, and Omani cooks often employ date derivatives like jam and syrup.

7.2 Well-liked Recipes and Street Cuisine

Shuwa: An integral part of Omani cuisine, Shuwa is a classic dish that is highly valued. Shuwa, a celebratory meal cooked in an underground sand oven, is made with marinated meat, usually goat or lamb, wrapped in banana leaves and cooked slowly. It is often made for special events. Tender, luscious flesh that tantalizes the senses is the product of the lengthy cooking procedure, which also adds a smoky taste.

Masoor Jareesh: Made from coarsely crushed wheat cooked with meat (often chicken or lamb) and seasoned with fragrant spices, Masoor Jareesh is a substantial and warming meal. This meal offers a pleasing combination of textures and tastes and symbolizes Oman's Bedouin tradition.

Mushaltat: A delicious flatbread stuffed with cheese, spicy meats, or a mix of the two, is a street food staple in Oman. Both residents and tourists prefer this tasty, portable snack while they're on the move. It's a tasty and handy delicacy with a crispy outside and flavorful inside.

Halwa: Omani Halwa is a delicious delicacy that carries cultural importance. Halwa, a sugary treat made with sugar, ghee, rosewater, and a variety of nuts, is often consumed at holidays and special events. The rich, luscious texture and careful preparation of Omani Halwa create a dessert that leaves a lasting impression on the mouth.

7.3 Table Manners

Dining in Oman is a cultural experience centered on hospitality, respect, and shared pleasure rather than simply the tastes on the plate. Gaining an understanding of Omani dining etiquette improves the whole gastronomic experience.

Communal Dining customs: Omani meals are often enjoyed communally, with sharing plates arranged in the middle of the table. This creates a feeling of community and invites visitors to participate in a shared experience. It is a show of warmth and charity to share meals.

Omani dining etiquette emphasizes the use of the right hand for eating, following the right-hand tradition. Although cutlery is often offered, it is preferred if guests feel at ease using their right hand to eat. Traditionally, the left hand is utilized for various duties and is seen to be less clean.

Generosity and Invitations: Oman is known for its warm hospitality, and visitors are often shown a great deal of generosity. Accepting offers to eat with locals is normal, and visitors are urged to say thank you for the meal. It is considered courteous to refuse seconds since it might be seen as a sign of dissatisfaction.

Tea and Coffee Rituals: As part of their hospitality, Omani people often provide tea or coffee to guests. These drinks are often served with dates. It is usual to accept offers of tea or coffee and to shake the cup or saucer politely as a sign of gratitude.

Respecting Cultural Sensitivities: It's best to dress modestly while eating with conservative hosts or in more formal situations. Furthermore, drinking alcohol is often only permitted in establishments with a license, so it's crucial to be aware of local laws and traditions.

To sum up, Omani food is more than just a menu; it's a window into the history, culture, and friendliness of the country. Every mouthful in Oman evokes a different memory, from rich meats slow-cooked in banana leaves to fragrant spice combinations. Indulging in Oman's gastronomic pleasures is an investigation of culture, hospitality, and the many tastes that characterize this captivating country, not merely a trip of the taste bud.

8. SHOPPING GUIDE

Oman, a country rich in cultural richness and history, provides a shopping experience that skillfully combines contemporary and traditional. This book explores Oman's retail scene, including everything from the nation's traditional souvenirs that represent its past to the busy Souq Al-Juma and the modern malls' attractiveness.

8.1 Customary Omani Keepsakes

Discovering Omani souvenirs is like taking a trip through the cultural core of the nation. Visitors may capture a little bit of Oman's rich heritage via handmade antiquities, elaborate linens, and traditional crafts.

Frankincense and Burners: Oman has long been the center of the frankincense trade and is still a major producer of premium frankincense. This aromatic resin is sold to visitors; it comes in different grades and is often paired with beautifully crafted burners. Crafted from clay or brass, the burners are ornamental as well as practical, signifying the country's long-standing ties to the priceless incense.

The Khanjar, also known as the Ceremonial Dagger, is a unique dagger with an elaborate hilt that has great cultural importance in Oman. The Khanjar, a sign of valor and honor, is often worn as a component of traditional clothing. Both little and bigger, more elaborate Khanjars are available to visitors, each showcasing the artistry and meaning of this well-known Omani trinket.

Bedouin crafts and silver jewelry: Omani silversmiths produce beautiful jewelry that combines traditional and modern patterns. An exquisite combination of semi precious stones, filigree work, and elaborate designs create bracelets, necklaces, and earrings that epitomize Omani artistry. Furthermore, Bedouin products like camel purses and weaved carpets provide an insight into nomadic lifestyles.

Omani Halwa: A beloved memento as well as a sweet treat for the palate, Omani Halwa is a candy. Halwa, when presented in colorful boxes, is a delightful and culturally meaningful gift. Common flavors include rosewater, saffron, and nuts, which provide a hint of Omani hospitality.

8.2 The Friday Market, or Souq Al-Juma

A visit to Souq Al-Juma, also known as the Friday Market, envelops guests in a lively and dynamic ambiance. Nestled between the seaside cities of Muscat and Sur, this ancient market is a veritable gold mine of regional goods, antiquities, and handicrafts.

Traditional Clothes and Textiles: Souq Al-Juma is well known for its extensive selection of traditional Omani clothing, which includes colorful scarves for ladies and embroidered dishdashas (men's robes). The intricate fabrics and designs that decorate these clothes, each of which reflects the distinctive regional fashions of many Omani communities, are open for exploration by guests.

Antiques & treasures: Vendors in Souq Al-Juma provide a wide range of treasures, including antique ceramics, old coins, and vintage silverware, making it a sanctuary for antique collectors. Every relic in these booths tells a tale about the cultural development of Oman, making an exploration seem like a trip into the past.

Local Fruits, Vegetables, and Spices: The fresh produce portion of the market is lively, with sellers showcasing locally produced fruits, vegetables, and spices. Guests may buy spices such as Omani frankincense, cardamom, and saffron and delight in the sensory pleasure of vivid hues and scents.

Artistry and Carpets: If you're looking for handcrafted rugs and carpets, Souq Al-Juma is the place to go. These works of art are distinguished by elaborate patterns, vivid colors, and traditional Bedouin motifs. There are carpets available in a range of sizes and designs, each of which narrates the story of Omani craftsmanship.

8.3 Up-to-Date Malls

Oman's contemporary malls provide a cutting-edge shopping experience that suits a wide range of preferences by skillfully fusing local flavors and global brands. These shopping centers, which are often found in large cities like Salalah, Sohar, and Muscat, provide a chic setting for window shopping.

Muscat Grand Mall: This shopping center is a shining example of Oman's adoption of modernism. A wide variety of local and worldwide brands offering fashion, technology, and lifestyle items can be found at this large shopping destination. The mall is a well-liked gathering place for both residents and visitors because of its many culinary selections and entertainment alternatives.

The Avenues Mall: Situated in Muscat, The Avenues Mall offers a distinctive fusion of upscale eating, shopping, and entertainment. This mall offers a plethora of luxury shops and worldwide fashion labels for people looking for an upscale shopping experience. It's a complete family attraction with its food court and recreational offerings.

Oman Avenues Mall: Located in the center of Muscat, Oman Avenues Mall blends leisure and entertainment with retail therapy. In addition to dining at a variety of restaurants and enjoying the many recreational amenities, visitors may peruse a blend of local and worldwide brands. A contemporary and welcoming ambiance is created by the mall's architecture and design.

Retail, entertainment, and eating are all integrated into Muscat City Centre, a destination for shopping and leisure. The mall serves a wide variety of customers with its varied selection of shops, which includes both local boutiques and international fashion brands. The whole experience is enhanced by the entertainment complex, which has family-friendly activities and a movie theater.

To sum up, Oman's retail scene presents an alluring fusion of history and contemporary design. Oman offers a wide variety of possibilities for visitors looking for retail experiences, from contemporary conveniences found in shopping malls to the busy Souq Al-Juma and traditional souvenirs that capture the nation's past. Whether browsing the aisles of a modern mall or navigating the winding lanes of a traditional souq, shopping in Oman offers a lively window into the country's rich cultural legacy and dynamic modern world.

9. HIDDEN GEMS

A nation of varied landscapes and age-old customs, Oman is rife with undiscovered treasures and off-the-beaten-path marvels just waiting to be discovered. These lesser-known locations provide a distinctive and genuine look into Oman's captivating spirit, from the historic appeal of Al Hamra Old Village to the natural wonder of Bimmah Sinkhole, the traditional craftsmanship of Sur's Dhow Factories, and the lush grandeur of Jebel Akhdar's Green Mountains.

9.1 Old Village of Al Hamra

A living example of Oman's rich cultural legacy, Al Hamra Old Village is tucked away against the Hajar Mountains. Tucked away from the hustle and bustle of the city, this ancient town welcomes guests to meander through its winding lanes and take in the spirit of traditional Omani architecture.

Historical Architecture: The well-preserved mud-brick buildings of Al Hamra Old Village are a famous example of a bygone era's architectural style. Some of the buildings are several hundred years old, and they have flat palm frond roofs, lattice windows, and elaborate wooden doors. The community offers a look into the environmentally friendly construction methods that have characterized Omani villages for many years.

Bait Al Safah Museum: This village-based museum provides a comprehensive exploration of Omani culture. The everyday life of Omani families is shown via interactive displays, historical exhibitions, and traditional artifacts. By introducing visitors to the rituals, traditions, and craftsmanship that characterize Al Hamra's history, the museum serves as a bridge between cultures.

Jebel Shams Viewpoint: Travelers may visit the neighboring Jebel Shams Viewpoint for expansive views of the surrounding area. The village's mud-brick homes shine in the warm tones as the sun sets over the Hajar Mountains, producing a lovely view. From this viewpoint, one may enjoy a calm and reflective view of Al Hamra's enduring allure.

9.2 Sinkhole at Bimmah

The Bimmah Sinkhole is a hidden natural marvel that enthralls with its unearthly beauty, close to the seaside resort of Dibba. Created when an underground cavern collapsed, this hidden jewel is now a surreal oasis that invites visitors to discover the magic of Oman's natural wonders.

Turquoise Waters: The blue waters of the Bimmah Sinkhole stand out sharply against the limestone cliffs that surround it. The sinkhole is a well-liked location for swimming and snorkeling because of its depth and transparency. The natural pool provides a cool respite from the Omani heat and is supplied by freshwater springs underneath.

Thick Foliage & Picnic Spots: There are shady spots for picnics and leisure all around the sinkhole thanks to the thick foliage that surrounds it. The tranquility of the surroundings allows visitors to relax in the natural atmosphere. The sinkhole is a peaceful haven due to its unusual mix of natural features and lush environs.

Cultural Beliefs and Legends: Those who live nearby regard the Bimmah Sinkhole to be a "well of offerings," and some even think that its waters have therapeutic qualities. The location is also rich in tradition, with stories of jinn and otherworldly beings lending this buried treasure an additional air of mystery. Examining the cultural stories associated with the sinkhole enhances the whole experience.

9.3 The Dhow Factories and Sur

Sur is a seaside town on Oman's eastern coast that is well-known for its nautical history and the art of dhow making. Away from the well-traveled tourist routes, Sur provides an opportunity to see the creativity and skill of Omani sailors, and its dhow factories serve as a reminder of the country's maritime heritage.

Dhow Building Yards: The Dhow building yards in Sur is a hidden gem, where master artisans carry on the long-standing custom of creating these classic wooden boats. Dhows are distinguished by their unique curving designs and have played a significant role in Oman's maritime history. Seeing the building process unfold, from cutting the wood to putting the pieces together, is an engrossing look into Omani maritime culture.

Ras Al Hadd Turtle Reserve: The Ras Al Hadd Turtle Reserve is located near Sur in Ras Al Hadd. Away from the bustle of the city, this quiet beach is home to green turtle breeding grounds. During the nesting season, the reserve offers guided excursions that provide a unique and personal wildlife experience, allowing visitors to see these magnificent birds in action.

The Sur Nautical Museum offers a more profound comprehension of Oman's nautical heritage. Displays highlight the development of navigational aids, shipbuilding methods, and the historical importance of Sur's shipyards. By introducing visitors to the seafaring customs that have created Oman's character, the museum acts as a cultural anchor.

9.4 The Green Mountains of Jebel Akhdar

Translated as "Green Mountain," Jebel Akhdar is a secret haven of verdant vistas and terraced fields nestled within the Al Hajar mountain range. This off-the-beaten-path location reveals the lush splendor of Oman's mountain refuge, providing a tranquil counterpoint to the parched lowlands.

Terraced Agriculture: The Green Mountains, with their historic terraces carved into the craggy cliffs, are a marvel of agricultural inventiveness. They are a patchwork of vivid vegetation. Pomegranates, apricots, and roses are just a few of the traditional agricultural techniques that guests may see. In addition to demonstrating human tenacity, the terraced fields provide a visual feast against the background of mountains.

Rose Harvesting Season: April is the time when the roses are harvested each year, and it's a stunning sight. Jebel Akhdar is well-known for its rose gardens. Rich, fragrant blooms of Damask roses turn the slope into a sea of pink petals. The harvest starts the process of producing Omani rose water, which is highly valued in the region's culinary arts and perfumes.

Villages with Scenery: Jebel Ak

10. TRAVEL ITINERARY

Travelers may enjoy a wide range of activities in Oman because of its unique combination of historic customs and stunning scenery. These example itineraries provide a carefully chosen roadmap for an enlightening trip across Oman's rich tapestry, regardless of your preferences for an exciting adventure, a grand tour that takes in the finest of the country, or a cultural immersion.

10.1 Immersion in Culture for 7 Days

Day 1: Getting to know Muscat

In the morning, take a tour of the magnificent Sultan Qaboos Grand Mosque.

Afternoon: Take a leisurely stroll around the lively Mutrah Souq and take in the lively ambiance of the bazaar.

Evening: Take a leisurely stroll along the Corniche and see the stunning waterfront views.

Day 2: Touring Muscat City

Visit the Royal Opera House in the morning, a cultural treasure that presents top-notch shows. Explore the National Museum of Oman in the afternoon, which provides insights into the rich history of the nation.

Evening: Enjoy a genuine Omani meal at a typical Omani restaurant.

Day 3: Travel to the Nizwa

Morning: Make your way to Nizwa and take in the breathtaking architecture of the old Nizwa Fort.

In the afternoon, explore the lively Nizwa Souq, which is well-known for its silverware and handicrafts.

Evening: Dine in the ancient town of Nizwa with a typical Omani cuisine.

Day 4: Jabal Shams and Al Hamra

In the morning, explore Al Hamra Old Village and take in the strikingly maintained mud-brick homes there.

In the afternoon, visit the "Mountain of the Sun," Jebel Shams, for some amazing vistas.

Evening: Take a nap in a mountain refuge and enjoy the starry sky.

Day 5: An Adventure in Wahiba Sands

Morning: Go dune bashing on an exhilarating desert tour at Wahiba Sands.

Afternoon: Take a camel ride at sundown and visit a Bedouin camp to get insight into their way of life.

Evening: For a genuine taste of the desert, spend the night camping outside.

Day 6: Sur's Coastal Exploration

Morning: Take a drive to Sur to see its dhow factory and observe the old-world workmanship.

See green turtles by visiting Ras Al Hadd Turtle Reserve in the afternoon.

Evening: Savor a seafood supper at Sam's waterfront.

Day 7: Leaving

Morning: Explore Sur's coastal attractions or go for a leisurely walk along the beach in the morning.

Afternoon: As you depart from Muscat International Airport, consider your experience with cultural immersion.

10.2 An Adventure Expedition Over Five Days

Day 1: Wadi Shab to Muscat

In the morning, take a drive to Wadi Shab and go climbing and swimming.

In the afternoon, see Wadi Shab's natural lakes and secret caverns.

Evening: Set a camp next to the wadi for a very engaging outdoor experience.

Day 2: Trekking Jebel Shams

After breakfast, set off for Jebel Shams, a strenuous hike along the edge of the "Grand Canyon of Arabia."

Afternoon: Savor a picnic lunch while taking in the expansive vistas of the untamed terrain.

Evening: Camp near Jebel Shams for a night of stargazing.

Day 3: Diving in the Daymaniyat Islands

Drive to the Daymaniyat Islands in the morning so you may spend the day diving in the magnificent marine reserve.

Explore the beautiful coral reefs and a variety of underwater habitats in the afternoon.

Evening: Spend a laid-back evening on the mainland.

Day 4: Safari at Wahiba Sands

Morning: Make your way to Wahiba Sands for a heart-pounding dune bashing adventure.

Visit a Bedouin camp in the afternoon for some sandboarding and cultural exchange.

Evening: Set a camp among the tall dunes in the center of Wahiba Sands.

Day 5: Ras Al Jinz Turtle Watching

In the morning, take a guided visit to Ras Al Jinz to see turtles.

In the afternoon, go along the coast and unwind on immaculate beaches.

Evening: Take in the enchanted spectacle of baby turtles migrating toward the ocean.

10.3 The 10-Day Grand Tour

Day 1–2: Touring Muscat

Discover the main attractions of Muscat, such as the Royal Opera House, Mutrah Souq, and Grand Mosque.

Savor authentic Omani food and take a leisurely stroll along the Corniche.

Day 3–4: Bahla and Nizwa

See the Souq and Nizwa Fort while learning about traditional crafts.

Explore the historic mud-brick walls of the Bahla Fort, which is classified by UNESCO.

Day 5–6: Al Hamra and Jebel Akhdar

Discover the verdant splendor of the tiered gardens of Jebel Akhdar.

Explore Al Hamra Old Village and enjoy sunset views from Jebel Shams.

Day 7–8: Sur's Coastal Adventures

Visit Sur's dhow industries and Turtle Reserve.

Enjoy the seaside atmosphere and unwind on Sur's beaches.

Day 9–10: Daymaniyat Islands and Wahiba Sands

Take a Bedouin tented experience and a desert safari at Wahiba Sands.

Dive into the underwater treasures of the Daymaniyat Islands.

These example itineraries provide an overview of the variety of experiences Oman has to offer, ranging from grand tours that capture the spirit of this captivating country to cultural immersion and adventure adventures. Oman's rich tapestry provides a voyage full of discovery and amazement, whether your interests lie in ancient monuments, natural marvels, or outdoor experiences.

11. USEFUL INFORMATION

Travelers are invited to discover Oman's attractions because of its hospitable culture, varied landscapes, and rich history. Knowing relevant information is essential to a smooth and pleasurable trip. With advice on everything from health and safety to handling money and communication, this book offers crucial information for a trouble-free trip in Oman.

11.1 Safety and Health Advice

Medical Planning: Although the healthcare system in Oman is well rated, it is still important to obtain comprehensive travel insurance that includes emergency medical coverage. Keep a basic first aid kit with necessary drugs with you at all times, particularly if you have any unique medical needs.

immunizations: Before visiting Oman, find out which immunizations are advised by your healthcare practitioner. It may be wise to get both routine and supplemental immunizations against illnesses like typhoid and hepatitis A.

Water and Food Safety: Although tap water is usually safe to drink in large cities, it's best to stick to bottled water, particularly in more isolated places. Be cautious while consuming street food, and make sure that heated meals are provided.

Sun Protection: The weather in Oman may be severe and there is a lot of sunshine. To shield yourself from the sun's rays, bring sunscreen, reapply it often, wear sunglasses, and drink plenty of water.

Respecting Local Customs: Given that Oman is a conservative nation, it's essential to observe local traditions and wear modest clothing, especially while visiting places of worship. Avoid public shows of love, particularly during the holy month of Ramadan.

Emergency Services: Get acquainted with the 999 emergency services number in Oman. Find out where the closest clinics or hospitals are as well, particularly if you're traveling through more isolated regions.

11.2 Money and Financial Issues

Currency: The Omani Rial (OMR) is the national currency of Oman. It's best to exchange money at banks or other locations that have been approved. In more traditional or rural settings, cash is favored; credit cards are generally accepted in metropolitan areas.

ATMs: Located mostly in cities and towns, ATMs provide a practical means of obtaining cash. To prevent any problems with transactions, make sure your credit or debit card is compatible with other countries and let your bank know when you will be traveling.

Tipping Etiquette: Although not required, tipping is respected in Oman, particularly in the service sector. A service fee might be added to the bill at restaurants. If not, it is usual to leave a gratuity that is between 5 and 10% of the whole amount.

Pricing Bargaining: While bargaining is popular in marketplaces and souqs, it is less common in malls and established stores. Being courteous is essential, and amiable bargaining may be a part of the cultural experience.

11.3 Interaction and Linkage

Language: Although English is generally known, particularly in tourist areas, hotels, and restaurants, Arabic is the official language of Oman. Acquiring a few fundamental Arabic words will improve your trip and demonstrate your appreciation for the way of life there.

Mobile networks and SIM cards: Purchasing a local SIM card is a great method to remain in touch when visiting Oman. Prepaid SIM cards are available from telecom companies like Omantel and Ooredoo with a range of data and call bundles. Good coverage is offered by mobile networks along major roads and in metropolitan areas.

Internet Access: Wi-Fi is available in the majority of metropolitan hotels, cafés, and shopping centers. However, connection could be spotty in more isolated places. Before heading out into less inhabited areas, think about downloading the essential applications and offline maps.

Postal Services: Post offices are located in most major cities in Oman, and the country has a dependable postal system. If you need to ship or receive items, there are also international courier services accessible.

Time Zone: Gulf Standard Time (GMT+4) is observed in Oman. Make careful to change your devices and calendar properly to the local time.

Electricity: 50Hz frequency and 240V standard voltage are the norm in Oman. Since type G outlets are widely used, if your equipment has a different plug type, make sure you have the required adapters with you.

In summary, having a solid awareness of the practical elements of traveling in Oman is critical to a seamless and pleasurable trip. These tips provide the groundwork for a fantastic trip to this alluring location in Arabia, covering everything from health and safety measures to handling money and maintaining communication. A mix of cultural understanding and practical preparation will enhance your journey in Oman, whether you're exploring tranquil scenery or navigating busy souqs.

12. APPENDIX

This appendix is a great way to enhance your travel experience as you set out on your adventure to Oman. These tips, which include helpful Arabic words, a thorough packing list, and crucial emergency contacts, will come in handy as you embark on your journey across this fascinating Arabian country.

12.1 Practical Arabic Phrases

Even though English is the most common language in Oman, people there value tourists who try to employ Arabic expressions. The following are helpful expressions to improve your interaction with others and your cultural knowledge:

Hi there: Salutations (السلام عليكم)

Farewell: May Allah be praised (مع السلامة)

Would you please: Fadlik Min (من فضلك)

Regards and thanks: Shukran (اكرًا)

Thank you very much: Afwan (عفوا)

Pardon me: 'Afuwan (to apologize) / Min fadlik (to attract attention) (من فضلك / عفوا)

Indeed, Na'am (نعم).

No, Laa ()

What is this worth? Kam hatha? (اذ؟ □)

Where is Ayna located? (أين)

Acquiring and using these expressions will not only promote effective communication but also demonstrate your admiration for Omani customs.

12.2 Inventory of Packing

You may increase the comfort and enjoyment of your trip by making sure you have the necessary materials packed. Before you go for Oman, be sure you check off the items on this checklist:

Clothes:

Lightweight and breathable materials for the hot heat.
Respect for local customs dictates modest attire, particularly while visiting places of worship.
cozy walking shoes for sightseeing.
The weather-Connected Products:

Sunscreen with high SPF.
Sunglasses and a wide-brimmed hat for sun protection.
Rain jacket that is breathable and lightweight, particularly if you are traveling during the rainy season.
Personal belongings:

Valid passport and appropriate travel documentation.

prescription drugs and a simple first aid package.

toiletries, such as wet wipes and hand sanitizer.

Connectivity and Technology:

adapters with power for your electronics.

A phone charger that you can carry about.

A worldwide SIM card or a local SIM card for communication.

Travel Add-ons:

cozy daypack suitable for travel.

Laundry detergent in travel-sized bottles for cleaning clothing

Maps and travel guidebooks.

Cash & Monetary:

Enough cash in the native currency (Omani Rial).

Debit and credit cards for purchases made in cities.

Other:

Using a smartphone or camera to record memories

If you want to visit coastal locations, bring snorkeling equipment.

Earplugs and a travel cushion allow for comfortable resting on lengthy flights.

Don't forget to modify this checklist according to the particular pursuits and areas of Oman that you want to visit.

12.3 Contacts for Emergencies

Although travel to Oman is typically secure, it's important to have emergency contacts on hand in case anything unexpected happens. For your own piece of mind, keep these numbers and addresses handy:

Services for Emergencies:

999 for the police
999 for an ambulance
Fire: 9999
Medical Support:

Muscat's Royal Hospital: +968 24 599 999
+968 24 446 666 Sultan Qaboos University Hospital (Muscat)
Consulates and embassies:

Your country's embassy or consulate in Oman. Make sure you have their address and phone number.
Travelers' Insurance:

Emergency contact number supplied by your travel insurance carrier.

Local Governments:

Tourism Police: (Oman toll-free) 8007-2222

Having these emergency contacts close at hand guarantees quick support in case of an unforeseen circumstance. For extra security, you should always disclose your trip schedule and lodging details to a dependable friend or relative.

Finally, this extensive appendix provides you with useful resources to improve your travel experience in Oman. These tools can help ensure a seamless and enjoyable journey, from learning some basic Arabic words to ensuring you have all the necessary packed and emergency contacts on hand. This book is an invaluable travel companion, whether you're touring historic forts, navigating busy souqs, or taking in Oman's breathtaking scenery.

Printed in Great Britain
by Amazon

39245199R00059